ENGINEERING

NOTEBOOK

NAME: _____

PHONE: _____

TABLE OF CONTENTS

PAGE	SUBJECT TITLE	DATE
1		
2		
3		
4		
5		
6		
7		
8		
9		
10		
11		
12		
13		
14		
15		
16		
17		
18		
19		
20		
21		
22		
23		
24		
25		
26		
27		
28		
29		
30		

TABLE OF CONTENTS

PAGE	SUBJECT TITLE	DATE
31		
32		
33		
34		
35		
36		
37		
38		
39		
40		
41		
42		
43		
44		
45		
46		
47		
48		
49		
50		
51		
52		
53		
54		
55		
56		
57		
58		
59		
60		

BOOK NO: _____

TABLE OF CONTENTS

PAGE	SUBJECT TITLE	DATE
61		
62		
63		
64		
65		
66		
67		
68		
69		
70		
71		
72		
73		
74		
75		
76		
77		
78		
79		
80		
81		
82		
83		
84		
85		
86		
87		
88		
89		
90		

TABLE OF CONTENTS

PAGE	SUBJECT TITLE	DATE
91		
92		
93		
94		
95		
96		
97		
98		
99		
100		
101		
102		
103		
104		
105		
106		
107		
108		
109		
110		
111		
112		
113		
114		
115		
116		
117		
118		
119		
120		

BOOK NO: _____

Continued from page

1

5

10

15

20

25

30

35

Continued to page

SINGNATURE   DATE

DISCLOSED TO AND UNDERSTOOD BY   DATE

PROPRIETARY INFORMATION

TITLE

PROJECT

Continued from page

2

5

10

15

20

25

30

35

Continued to page

SINGNATURE

DATE

DISCLOSED TO AND UNDERSTOOD BY

DATE

PROPRIETARY INFORMATION

TITLE

PROJECT

Continued from page

3

5

10

15

20

25

30

35

Continued to page

SINGNATURE

DATE

DISCLOSED TO AND UNDERSTOOD BY

DATE

PROPRIETARY INFORMATION

TITLE

PROJECT

Continued from page

4

5

10

15

20

25

30

35

Continued to page

SINGNATURE

DATE

DISCLOSED TO AND UNDERSTOOD BY

DATE

PROPRIETARY INFORMATION

Continued from page

5

5

10

15

20

25

30

35

Continued to page

SINGNATURE

DATE

DISCLOSED TO AND UNDERSTOOD BY

DATE

PROPRIETARY INFORMATION

TITLE

PROJECT

Continued from page

6

5

10

15

20

25

30

35

Continued to page

SINGNATURE

DATE

DISCLOSED TO AND UNDERSTOOD BY

DATE

PROPRIETARY INFORMATION

Continued from page

7

5

10

15

20

25

30

35

Continued to page

SINGNATURE | DATE

DISCLOSED TO AND UNDERSTOOD BY | DATE

PROPRIETARY INFORMATION

Continued from page

8

5

10

15

20

25

30

35

Continued to page

SINGNATURE

DATE

DISCLOSED TO AND UNDERSTOOD BY

DATE

PROPRIETARY INFORMATION

TITLE

PROJECT

Continued from page

9

5

10

15

20

25

30

35

Continued to page

SINGNATURE

DATE

DISCLOSED TO AND UNDERSTOOD BY

DATE

PROPRIETARY INFORMATION

Continued from page

10

5

10

15

20

25

30

35

Continued to page

SINGNATURE   DATE

DISCLOSED TO AND UNDERSTOOD BY   DATE

PROPRIETARY INFORMATION

Continued from page

11

5

10

15

20

25

30

35

Continued to page

SINGNATURE

DATE

DISCLOSED TO AND UNDERSTOOD BY

DATE

PROPRIETARY INFORMATION

TITLE

PROJECT

Continued from page

12

5

10

15

20

25

30

35

Continued to page

SINGNATURE

DATE

DISCLOSED TO AND UNDERSTOOD BY

DATE

PROPRIETARY INFORMATION

Continued from page

13

5

10

15

20

25

30

35

Continued to page

SINGNATURE   DATE

DISCLOSED TO AND UNDERSTOOD BY   DATE

PROPRIETARY INFORMATION

Continued from page

5

10

15

20

25

30

35

Continued to page

SINGNATURE

DATE

DISCLOSED TO AND UNDERSTOOD BY

DATE

PROPRIETARY INFORMATION

Continued from page

5

10

15

20

25

30

35

Continued to page

SINGNATURE   DATE

DISCLOSED TO AND UNDERSTOOD BY   DATE

PROPRIETARY INFORMATION

Continued from page

5

10

15

20

25

30

35

Continued to page

SINGNATURE   DATE

DISCLOSED TO AND UNDERSTOOD BY   DATE

PROPRIETARY INFORMATION

Continued from page

5

10

15

20

25

30

35

Continued to page

SINGNATURE   DATE

DISCLOSED TO AND UNDERSTOOD BY   DATE

PROPRIETARY INFORMATION

TITLE

PROJECT

Continued from page

18

5

10

15

20

25

30

35

Continued to page

SINGNATURE

DATE

DISCLOSED TO AND UNDERSTOOD BY

DATE

PROPRIETARY INFORMATION

Continued from page

5

10

15

20

25

30

35

Continued to page

SINGNATURE

DATE

DISCLOSED TO AND UNDERSTOOD BY

DATE

PROPRIETARY INFORMATION

Continued from page

Continued to page

SINGNATURE

DATE

DISCLOSED TO AND UNDERSTOOD BY

DATE

PROPRIETARY INFORMATION

Continued from page

5

10

15

20

25

30

35

Continued to page

SINGNATURE

DATE

DISCLOSED TO AND UNDERSTOOD BY

DATE

PROPRIETARY INFORMATION

Continued from page

22

5

10

15

20

25

30

35

Continued to page

SINGNATURE   DATE

DISCLOSED TO AND UNDERSTOOD BY   DATE

PROPRIETARY INFORMATION

Continued from page

23

5

10

15

20

25

30

35

Continued to page

SINGNATURE

DATE

DISCLOSED TO AND UNDERSTOOD BY

DATE

PROPRIETARY INFORMATION

Continued from page

24

5

10

15

20

25

30

35

Continued to page

SINGNATURE

DATE

DISCLOSED TO AND UNDERSTOOD BY

DATE

PROPRIETARY INFORMATION

Continued from page

5

10

15

20

25

30

35

Continued to page

SINGNATURE

DATE

DISCLOSED TO AND UNDERSTOOD BY

DATE

PROPRIETARY INFORMATION

Continued from page

5

10

15

20

25

30

35

Continued to page

SINGNATURE

DATE

DISCLOSED TO AND UNDERSTOOD BY

DATE

PROPRIETARY INFORMATION

Continued from page

5

10

15

20

25

30

35

Continued to page

SINGNATURE   DATE

DISCLOSED TO AND UNDERSTOOD BY   DATE

PROPRIETARY INFORMATION

Continued from page

28

5

10

15

20

25

30

35

Continued to page

SINGNATURE

DATE

DISCLOSED TO AND UNDERSTOOD BY

DATE

PROPRIETARY INFORMATION

Continued from page

Continued to page

5

10

15

20

25

30

35

SINGNATURE

DATE

DISCLOSED TO AND UNDERSTOOD BY

DATE

PROPRIETARY INFORMATION

Continued from page

30

5

10

15

20

25

30

35

Continued to page

SINGNATURE DATE

DISCLOSED TO AND UNDERSTOOD BY DATE

PROPRIETARY INFORMATION

TITLE   PROJECT

Continued from page

31

5

10

15

20

25

30

35

Continued to page

SINGNATURE   DATE

DISCLOSED TO AND UNDERSTOOD BY   DATE

PROPRIETARY INFORMATION

TITLE

PROJECT

Continued from page

32

5

10

15

20

25

30

35

Continued to page

SINGNATURE

DATE

DISCLOSED TO AND UNDERSTOOD BY

DATE

PROPRIETARY INFORMATION

Continued from page

5

10

15

20

25

30

35

Continued to page

SINGNATURE

DATE

DISCLOSED TO AND UNDERSTOOD BY

DATE

PROPRIETARY INFORMATION

Continued from page

34

5

10

15

20

25

30

35

Continued to page

SINGNATURE　　　　　　　　　　　　　　　　DATE

DISCLOSED TO AND UNDERSTOOD BY　　　　　DATE

PROPRIETARY INFORMATION

Continued from page

35

5

10

15

20

25

30

35

Continued to page

SINGNATURE   DATE

DISCLOSED TO AND UNDERSTOOD BY   DATE

PROPRIETARY INFORMATION

Continued from page

36

5

10

15

20

25

30

35

Continued to page

SINGNATURE

DATE

DISCLOSED TO AND UNDERSTOOD BY

DATE

PROPRIETARY INFORMATION

Continued from page

5

10

15

20

25

30

35

Continued to page

SINGNATURE

DATE

DISCLOSED TO AND UNDERSTOOD BY

DATE

PROPRIETARY INFORMATION

Continued from page

38

5

10

15

20

25

30

35

Continued to page

SINGNATURE

DATE

DISCLOSED TO AND UNDERSTOOD BY

DATE

PROPRIETARY INFORMATION

Continued from page

5

10

15

20

25

30

35

Continued to page

SINGNATURE

DATE

DISCLOSED TO AND UNDERSTOOD BY

DATE

PROPRIETARY INFORMATION

Continued from page

40

5

10

15

20

25

30

35

Continued to page

SINGNATURE

DATE

DISCLOSED TO AND UNDERSTOOD BY

DATE

PROPRIETARY INFORMATION

Continued from page

5

10

15

20

25

30

35

Continued to page

SINGNATURE

DATE

DISCLOSED TO AND UNDERSTOOD BY

DATE

Continued from page

42

5

10

15

20

25

30

35

Continued to page

SINGNATURE   DATE

DISCLOSED TO AND UNDERSTOOD BY   DATE

PROPRIETARY INFORMATION

Continued from page

5

10

15

20

25

30

35

Continued to page

SINGNATURE   DATE

DISCLOSED TO AND UNDERSTOOD BY   DATE

PROPRIETARY INFORMATION

Continued from page

44

5

10

15

20

25

30

35

Continued to page

SINGNATURE

DATE

DISCLOSED TO AND UNDERSTOOD BY

DATE

PROPRIETARY INFORMATION

Continued from page

45

5

10

15

20

25

30

35

Continued to page

SINGNATURE   DATE

DISCLOSED TO AND UNDERSTOOD BY   DATE

PROPRIETARY INFORMATION

Continued from page

5

10

15

20

25

30

35

Continued to page

SINGNATURE

DATE

DISCLOSED TO AND UNDERSTOOD BY

DATE

PROPRIETARY INFORMATION

Continued from page

47

Continued to page

SINGNATURE

DATE

DISCLOSED TO AND UNDERSTOOD BY

DATE

PROPRIETARY INFORMATION

TITLE

PROJECT

Continued from page

48

5

10

15

20

25

30

35

Continued to page

SINGNATURE

DATE

DISCLOSED TO AND UNDERSTOOD BY

DATE

PROPRIETARY INFORMATION

Continued from page

49

5

10

15

20

25

30

35

Continued to page

SINGNATURE

DATE

DISCLOSED TO AND UNDERSTOOD BY

DATE

PROPRIETARY INFORMATION

Continued from page

50

5

10

15

20

25

30

35

Continued to page

SINGNATURE

DATE

DISCLOSED TO AND UNDERSTOOD BY

DATE

PROPRIETARY INFORMATION

Continued from page

51

5

10

15

20

25

30

35

Continued to page

SINGNATURE

DATE

DISCLOSED TO AND UNDERSTOOD BY

DATE

PROPRIETARY INFORMATION

Continued from page

5

10

15

20

25

30

35

Continued to page

SINGNATURE

DATE

DISCLOSED TO AND UNDERSTOOD BY

DATE

PROPRIETARY INFORMATION

Continued from page

53

5

10

15

20

25

30

35

Continued to page

SINGNATURE

DATE

DISCLOSED TO AND UNDERSTOOD BY

DATE

PROPRIETARY INFORMATION

TITLE

PROJECT

Continued from page

54

5

10

15

20

25

30

35

Continued to page

SINGNATURE

DATE

DISCLOSED TO AND UNDERSTOOD BY

DATE

PROPRIETARY INFORMATION

Continued from page

55

5

10

15

20

25

30

35

Continued to page

SINGNATURE

DATE

DISCLOSED TO AND UNDERSTOOD BY

DATE

PROPRIETARY INFORMATION

Continued from page

56

5

10

15

20

25

30

35

Continued to page

SINGNATURE

DATE

DISCLOSED TO AND UNDERSTOOD BY

DATE

PROPRIETARY INFORMATION

Continued from page

57

5

10

15

20

25

30

35

Continued to page

SINGNATURE

DATE

DISCLOSED TO AND UNDERSTOOD BY

DATE

PROPRIETARY INFORMATION

5

10

15

20

25

30

35

Continued to page

SINGNATURE

DATE

DISCLOSED TO AND UNDERSTOOD BY

DATE

PROPRIETARY INFORMATION

Continued from page

59

5

10

15

20

25

30

35

Continued to page

SINGNATURE   DATE

DISCLOSED TO AND UNDERSTOOD BY   DATE

PROPRIETARY INFORMATION

Continued from page

60

5

10

15

20

25

30

35

Continued to page

SINGNATURE   DATE

DISCLOSED TO AND UNDERSTOOD BY   DATE

PROPRIETARY INFORMATION

Continued from page

5

10

15

20

25

30

35

Continued to page

SINGNATURE

DATE

DISCLOSED TO AND UNDERSTOOD BY

DATE

PROPRIETARY INFORMATION

5

10

15

20

25

30

35

Continued to page

SINGNATURE

DATE

DISCLOSED TO AND UNDERSTOOD BY

DATE

PROPRIETARY INFORMATION

Continued from page

63

5

10

15

20

25

30

35

Continued to page

SINGNATURE   DATE

DISCLOSED TO AND UNDERSTOOD BY   DATE

PROPRIETARY INFORMATION

Continued from page

5

10

15

20

25

30

35

Continued to page

SINGNATURE

DATE

DISCLOSED TO AND UNDERSTOOD BY

DATE

PROPRIETARY INFORMATION

Continued from page

5

10

15

20

25

30

35

Continued to page

SINGNATURE

DATE

DISCLOSED TO AND UNDERSTOOD BY

DATE

PROPRIETARY INFORMATION

Continued from page

5

10

15

20

25

30

35

Continued to page

SINGNATURE

DATE

DISCLOSED TO AND UNDERSTOOD BY

DATE

PROPRIETARY INFORMATION

Continued from page

67

5

10

15

20

25

30

35

Continued to page

SINGNATURE   DATE

DISCLOSED TO AND UNDERSTOOD BY   DATE

PROPRIETARY INFORMATION

Continued from page

68

5

10

15

20

25

30

35

Continued to page

SINGNATURE   DATE

DISCLOSED TO AND UNDERSTOOD BY   DATE

PROPRIETARY INFORMATION

Continued from page

5

10

15

20

25

30

35

Continued to page

SINGNATURE

DATE

DISCLOSED TO AND UNDERSTOOD BY

DATE

PROPRIETARY INFORMATION

Continued from page

70

5

10

15

20

25

30

35

Continued to page

SINGNATURE

DATE

DISCLOSED TO AND UNDERSTOOD BY

DATE

PROPRIETARY INFORMATION

Continued from page

71

5

10

15

20

25

30

35

Continued to page

SINGNATURE   DATE

DISCLOSED TO AND UNDERSTOOD BY   DATE

PROPRIETARY INFORMATION

Continued from page

72

5

10

15

20

25

30

35

Continued to page

SINGNATURE

DATE

DISCLOSED TO AND UNDERSTOOD BY

DATE

PROPRIETARY INFORMATION

Continued from page

Continued to page

SINGNATURE　　　　　　　　　　　　　　　DATE

DISCLOSED TO AND UNDERSTOOD BY　　　　　DATE

PROPRIETARY INFORMATION

5

10

15

20

25

30

35

Continued from page

74

5

10

15

20

25

30

35

Continued to page

SINGNATURE   DATE

DISCLOSED TO AND UNDERSTOOD BY   DATE

PROPRIETARY INFORMATION

Continued from page

5

10

15

20

25

30

35

Continued to page

SINGNATURE

DATE

DISCLOSED TO AND UNDERSTOOD BY

DATE

PROPRIETARY INFORMATION

Continued from page

76

5

10

15

20

25

30

35

Continued to page

SINGNATURE

DATE

DISCLOSED TO AND UNDERSTOOD BY

DATE

PROPRIETARY INFORMATION

Continued from page

5

10

15

20

25

30

35

Continued to page

SINGNATURE   DATE

DISCLOSED TO AND UNDERSTOOD BY   DATE

PROPRIETARY INFORMATION

Continued from page

5

10

15

20

25

30

35

Continued to page

SINGNATURE

DATE

DISCLOSED TO AND UNDERSTOOD BY

DATE

PROPRIETARY INFORMATION

Continued from page

5

10

15

20

25

30

35

Continued to page

SINGNATURE

DATE

DISCLOSED TO AND UNDERSTOOD BY

DATE

PROPRIETARY INFORMATION

Continued from page

80

5

10

15

20

25

30

35

Continued to page

SINGNATURE   DATE

DISCLOSED TO AND UNDERSTOOD BY   DATE

PROPRIETARY INFORMATION

TITLE　　　　　　　　　　　PROJECT

Continued from page

81

5

10

15

20

25

30

35

Continued to page

SINGNATURE　　　　　　　　　　　　　　　　DATE

DISCLOSED TO AND UNDERSTOOD BY　　　　　　DATE

PROPRIETARY INFORMATION

TITLE

PROJECT

Continued from page

82

5

10

15

20

25

30

35

Continued to page

SINGNATURE

DATE

DISCLOSED TO AND UNDERSTOOD BY

DATE

PROPRIETARY INFORMATION

Continued from page

5

10

15

20

25

30

35

Continued to page

SINGNATURE

DATE

DISCLOSED TO AND UNDERSTOOD BY

DATE

PROPRIETARY INFORMATION

Continued from page

5

10

15

20

25

30

35

Continued to page

SINGNATURE

DATE

DISCLOSED TO AND UNDERSTOOD BY

DATE

PROPRIETARY INFORMATION

Continued from page

85

5

10

15

20

25

30

35

Continued to page

SINGNATURE

DATE

DISCLOSED TO AND UNDERSTOOD BY

DATE

PROPRIETARY INFORMATION

Continued from page

5

10

15

20

25

30

35

Continued to page

SINGNATURE

DATE

DISCLOSED TO AND UNDERSTOOD BY

DATE

TITLE

PROJECT

Continued from page

87

5

10

15

20

25

30

35

Continued to page

SINGNATURE

DATE

DISCLOSED TO AND UNDERSTOOD BY

DATE

PROPRIETARY INFORMATION

Continued from page

5

10

15

20

25

30

35

Continued to page

SINGNATURE

DATE

DISCLOSED TO AND UNDERSTOOD BY

DATE

PROPRIETARY INFORMATION

TITLE

PROJECT

Continued from page

89

5

10

15

20

25

30

35

Continued to page

SINGNATURE

DATE

DISCLOSED TO AND UNDERSTOOD BY

DATE

PROPRIETARY INFORMATION

Continued from page

5

10

15

20

25

30

35

Continued to page

SINGNATURE

DATE

DISCLOSED TO AND UNDERSTOOD BY

DATE

PROPRIETARY INFORMATION

Continued from page

5

10

15

20

25

30

35

Continued to page

SINGNATURE   DATE

DISCLOSED TO AND UNDERSTOOD BY   DATE

PROPRIETARY INFORMATION

TITLE   PROJECT

Continued from page

92

5

10

15

20

25

30

35

Continued to page

SINGNATURE   DATE

DISCLOSED TO AND UNDERSTOOD BY   DATE

PROPRIETARY INFORMATION

Continued from page

Continued to page

SINGNATURE

DATE

DISCLOSED TO AND UNDERSTOOD BY

DATE

PROPRIETARY INFORMATION

Continued from page

5

10

15

20

25

30

35

Continued to page

SINGNATURE

DATE

DISCLOSED TO AND UNDERSTOOD BY

DATE

PROPRIETARY INFORMATION

Continued from page

95

5

10

15

20

25

30

35

Continued to page

SINGNATURE   DATE

DISCLOSED TO AND UNDERSTOOD BY   DATE

PROPRIETARY INFORMATION

Continued from page

5

10

15

20

25

30

35

Continued to page

SINGNATURE

DATE

DISCLOSED TO AND UNDERSTOOD BY

DATE

PROPRIETARY INFORMATION

Continued from page

97

5

10

15

20

25

30

35

Continued to page

SINGNATURE

DATE

DISCLOSED TO AND UNDERSTOOD BY

DATE

PROPRIETARY INFORMATION

Continued from page

5

10

15

20

25

30

35

Continued to page

SINGNATURE

DATE

DISCLOSED TO AND UNDERSTOOD BY

DATE

PROPRIETARY INFORMATION

TITLE   PROJECT

Continued from page

99

5

10

15

20

25

30

35

Continued to page

SINGNATURE   DATE

DISCLOSED TO AND UNDERSTOOD BY   DATE

PROPRIETARY INFORMATION

5

10

15

20

25

30

35

Continued to page

SINGNATURE

DATE

DISCLOSED TO AND UNDERSTOOD BY

DATE

PROPRIETARY INFORMATION

Continued from page

5

10

15

20

25

30

35

Continued to page

SINGNATURE   DATE

DISCLOSED TO AND UNDERSTOOD BY   DATE

PROPRIETARY INFORMATION

Continued from page

5

10

15

20

25

30

35

Continued to page

SINGNATURE

DATE

DISCLOSED TO AND UNDERSTOOD BY

DATE

PROPRIETARY INFORMATION

Continued from page

103

5

10

15

20

25

30

35

Continued to page

SINGNATURE   DATE

DISCLOSED TO AND UNDERSTOOD BY   DATE

PROPRIETARY INFORMATION

Continued from page

104

5

10

15

20

25

30

35

Continued to page

SINGNATURE   DATE

DISCLOSED TO AND UNDERSTOOD BY   DATE

PROPRIETARY INFORMATION

Continued from page

| | 5 |
| 10 |
| 15 |
| 20 |
| 25 |
| 30 |
| 35 |

Continued to page

SINGNATURE

DATE

DISCLOSED TO AND UNDERSTOOD BY

DATE

PROPRIETARY INFORMATION

Continued from page

5

10

15

20

25

30

35

Continued to page

SINGNATURE

DATE

DISCLOSED TO AND UNDERSTOOD BY

DATE

PROPRIETARY INFORMATION

Continued from page

5

10

15

20

25

30

35

Continued to page

SINGNATURE | DATE

DISCLOSED TO AND UNDERSTOOD BY | DATE

PROPRIETARY INFORMATION

Continued from page

108

5

10

15

20

25

30

35

Continued to page

SINGNATURE   DATE

DISCLOSED TO AND UNDERSTOOD BY   DATE

PROPRIETARY INFORMATION

Continued from page

109

Continued to page

SINGNATURE DATE

DISCLOSED TO AND UNDERSTOOD BY DATE

PROPRIETARY INFORMATION

TITLE

PROJECT

Continued from page

110

5

10

15

20

25

30

35

Continued to page

SINGNATURE

DATE

DISCLOSED TO AND UNDERSTOOD BY

DATE

PROPRIETARY INFORMATION

Continued from page

5

10

15

20

25

30

35

Continued to page

SINGNATURE

DATE

DISCLOSED TO AND UNDERSTOOD BY

DATE

PROPRIETARY INFORMATION

Continued from page

112

5

10

15

20

25

30

35

Continued to page

SINGNATURE   DATE

DISCLOSED TO AND UNDERSTOOD BY   DATE

PROPRIETARY INFORMATION

Continued from page

113

5

10

15

20

25

30

35

Continued to page

SINGNATURE   DATE

DISCLOSED TO AND UNDERSTOOD BY   DATE

PROPRIETARY INFORMATION

Continued from page

114

5

10

15

20

25

30

35

Continued to page

SINGNATURE

DATE

DISCLOSED TO AND UNDERSTOOD BY

DATE

PROPRIETARY INFORMATION

Continued from page

115

5

10

15

20

25

30

35

Continued to page

SINGNATURE   DATE

DISCLOSED TO AND UNDERSTOOD BY   DATE

PROPRIETARY INFORMATION

Continued from page

5

10

15

20

25

30

35

Continued to page

SINGNATURE

DATE

DISCLOSED TO AND UNDERSTOOD BY

DATE

PROPRIETARY INFORMATION

Continued from page

5

10

15

20

25

30

35

Continued to page

SINGNATURE   DATE

DISCLOSED TO AND UNDERSTOOD BY   DATE

PROPRIETARY INFORMATION

Continued from page

118

5

10

15

20

25

30

35

Continued to page

SINGNATURE   DATE

DISCLOSED TO AND UNDERSTOOD BY   DATE

PROPRIETARY INFORMATION

Continued from page

119

5

10

15

20

25

30

35

Continued to page

SINGNATURE

DATE

DISCLOSED TO AND UNDERSTOOD BY

DATE

PROPRIETARY INFORMATION

Continued from page

5

10

15

20

25

30

35

Continued to page

SINGNATURE

DATE

DISCLOSED TO AND UNDERSTOOD BY

DATE

PROPRIETARY INFORMATION

Made in United States
Troutdale, OR
02/26/2024

17995667R00071